WORLD ALMANAC®
LIBRARY OF THE STATES

Michigan

THE WOLVERINE STATE

by Rachel Barenblat

Curriculum Consultant: Jean Craven,
Director of Instructional Support,
Albuquerque, NM, Public Schools

WORLD ALMANAC® LIBRARY

Please visit our web site at: **www.worldalmanaclibrary.com**
For a free color catalog describing World Almanac® Library's list of high-quality books
and multimedia programs, call 1-800-848-2928 or fax your request to (414) 332-3567.

Library of Congress Cataloging-in-Publication Data

Barenblat, Rachel.
 Michigan, the Wolverine State / by Rachel Barenblat.
  p. cm. — (World Almanac Library of the states)
 Includes bibliographical references and index.
 Summary: Illustrations and text present the history, geography, people, politics and
government, economy, and social life and customs of Michigan, which is the only state
to touch four of the five Great Lakes.
 ISBN 0-8368-5117-X (lib. bdg.)
 ISBN 0-8368-5287-7 (softcover)
 1. Michigan—Juvenile literature. [1. Michigan.] I. Title. II. Series.
 F566.3.B37 2002
 977.4—dc21   2001046987

This edition first published in 2002 by
World Almanac® Library
330 West Olive Street, Suite 100
Milwaukee, WI 53212 USA

Design and Editorial: **Jack&Bill**/Bill SMITH STUDIO Inc.
Editors: Jackie Ball and Kristen Behrens
Art Directors: Ron Leighton and Jeffrey Rutzky
Photo Research and Buying: Christie Silver and Sean Livingstone
Design and Production: Maureen O'Connor and Jeffrey Rutzky
World Almanac® Library Editors: Patricia Lantier, Amy Stone, Valerie J. Weber,
Catherine Gardner, Carolyn Kott Washburne, Alan Wachtel, Monica Rausch
World Almanac® Library Production: Scott M. Krall, Eva Erato-Rudek, Tammy Gruenewald,
Katherine A. Goedheer

Photo credits: pp. 4, 6 © Corel; p. 7 (all) © PhotoDisc; p. 9 © Corel; p. 10 © David F. Wisse;
p. 11 © ArtToday; p. 12 © Corel; p. 13 © ArtToday; p. 14 © Corel; p. 15 © Dover Publications;
p. 17 © Painet; p. 18 © PhotoDisc; p. 19 © Crystal Mountain Resort; p. 20 (from left to right)
© Vito Palmisano, © Grand Traverse CVB, © Thomas A. Schneider; p. 21 (all) courtesy of
Travel Michigan; p. 22 © Painet; p. 26 (top) © PhotoDisc, (left) © James Keyser/TimePix;
p. 27 © PhotoDisc; p. 29 courtesy of Travel Michigan; p. 31 (top) © Corel, (bottom) © Library
of Congress; p. 32 © Library of Congress; p. 33 courtesy of Travel Michigan; p. 34 © Steve
Kagan/TimePix; p. 35 © Corel; p. 36 (top) courtesy of Travel Michigan, (bottom) © Jeffrey
Rutzky; p. 37 (top) © Randall McCune, (bottom) © Library of Congress; p. 38 © ArtToday;
p. 39 (top) © Library of Congress, (bottom) © ArtToday; p. 40 (clockwise) © Artville, © Artville,
© Artville, © Dover Publications; p. 41 © Ann Clifford; pp. 42–43 © Library of Congress;
p. 44 (clockwise) © Jeffrey Rutzky, © Raymond J. Malace, © Corel; p. 45 (top) © Vito
Palmisano, (bottom) © PhotoDisc

Printed in the United States of America

1 2 3 4 5 6 7 8 9 06 05 04 03 02

Michigan

Boom and Bust

No point in Michigan is more than 85 miles (136 kilometers) from one of the four Great Lakes — Michigan, Superior, Huron, and Erie — that touch Michigan's shores. Water also marks the dividing line between two ways of life. Lake Michigan separates the state's Lower and Upper Peninsulas. More urban, the Lower Peninsula is strongly tied to the state's manufacturing base, particularly the manufacture of cars. By 1925 Detroit, the state's first capital, was home to the "Big Three" car manufacturers in the United States — General Motors, Ford, and Chrysler. This trend began in 1908, when the first of Henry Ford's Model As rolled off the assembly line. But Michigan's close association with the automotive industry precedes even Ford's great accomplishment. P. F. Olds of Lansing was a successful engineer and inventor who developed a working automobile engine. In 1896 he and his son created one of the first working passenger vehicles. It was this success that focused the automotive industry's interest on Michigan, and the rest, as they say, is history.

The industrial success of the Lower Peninsula is at odds with the agricultural base of the Upper Peninsula. Home to only 3 percent of Michigan's population, the area relies primarily on dairy farming and the logging industry for income. Far from the center of political and economic power, Michiganders here have sometimes talked of seceding and forming their own state or of joining neighboring Wisconsin, a state with a more agrarian economy.

The economic bases of both the Upper and Lower Peninsulas are similar in at least one way, however — both are tightly tied to the economy of the nation as a whole. The logging and automotive industries experience cycles of stellar heights and deep lows, the effects of which resound throughout the state.

▶ Map of Michigan showing the interstate highway system, as well as major cities and waterways.

▼ 1919 Ford Model T.

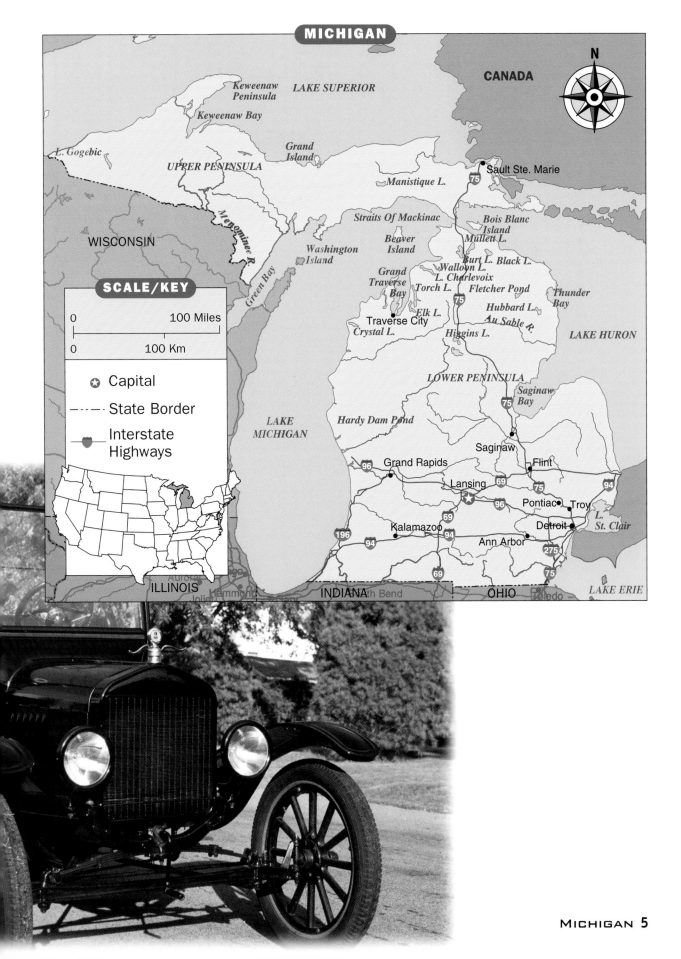

N

CANADA

LAKE SUPERIOR

Keweenaw
Peninsula

Keweenaw Bay

L. Gogebic

UPPER PENINSULA

Grand
Island

Manistique L.

Sault Ste. Marie

75

WISCONSIN

Menominee R.

Green Bay

Washington
Island

Straits Of Mackinac

Beaver
Island

Bois Blanc
Island
Mullett L.

Burt L. Black L.
Walloon L.
L. Charlevoix
Fletcher Pond

Thunder
Bay

Grand
Traverse
Bay
Torch L.

75

Hubbard L.
Au Sable R.

LAKE HURON

Elk L.
Traverse City
Crystal L.

Higgins L.

LOWER PENINSULA

Saginaw
Bay

75

LAKE
MICHIGAN

Hardy Dam Pond

Saginaw

Grand Rapids

96

Flint

Lansing

69

75

94

196

Kalamazoo

69

94

Pontiac   Troy
96
L.
St. Clair

Detroit

Ann Arbor

275

ILLINOIS

INDIANA   South Bend

69

94

75

OHIO

LAKE ERIE

Fast Facts

MICHIGAN (MI), Wolverine State, Great Lakes State

Entered Union
January 26, 1837 (26th state)

Capital
Lansing 119,128
Population

Total Population (2000)
9,938,444 (8th most populous state)

Largest Cities — Population
Detroit 951,270
Grand Rapids 197,800
Warren 138,247
Flint 124,943
Sterling Heights 124,471

Land Area
56,804 square miles (147,122 square kilometers) (22nd largest state)

State Motto
Si quaeris peninsulam amoenam, circumspice *(If you seek a pleasant peninsula, look about you.)*

State Song
"Michigan, My Michigan" *by William Otto Miessner and Douglas M. Malloch*

State Game Mammal
White-tailed Deer

State Bird
Robin — *In mid-March the first flash of the male robin's red breast is hailed as the unofficial harbinger of spring.*

State Fish
Brook Trout

State Reptile
Painted Turtle — *Only twenty of the nation's fifty states have adopted state reptiles. Four have state amphibians.*

State Tree
White Pine

State Flower
Apple Blossom — *"You take the fruit, we'll take the flower." The apple might be New York's state fruit, but the fragrant apple blossom is Michigan's state flower. State lore claims that old Johnny Appleseed himself first planted apple trees in Michigan.*

State Wildflower
Dwarf Lake Iris

State Gem
Isle Royale Greenstone

State Soil
Kalkaska Soil Series

State Stone
Petoskey Stone — *Michigan's state stone once lay at the bottom of the ocean. The stone is in fact fossilized colony corals from the Devonian seas that covered lower Michigan about 350 years ago. Now, Petoskey stones can be found on beaches and in gravel pits and ditches all over Michigan.*

PLACES TO VISIT

Pictured Rocks National Lakeshore

Pictured Rocks is the name given to a set of cliff formations of Cambrian sandstone. They were the home place of the gods of thunder and lightning in Henry Wadsworth Longfellow's poem "The Song of Hiawatha."

Sault Ste. Marie

The city of Sault Ste. Marie, located on the rapids of the St. Marys River, is known as the "Soo." Its first set of locks to bypass the river's rapids went into operation in 1855. The locks raise or lower vessels 21 feet (6 meters) above the rapids in six to fifteen minutes.

Upper Peninsula

In the Upper Peninsula of Michigan, called the "UP" by locals, hike in gently rolling hills, fish in freshwater streams, or, in the wintertime, learn to make ice sculptures and cross-country ski!

For other places and events to attend, see p. 44.

BIGGEST, BEST, AND MOST

- It is the only state that touches four of the five Great Lakes.
- It has the world's longest freshwater shoreline.

STATE FIRSTS

- Michigan was the first state to provide for the establishment of public libraries.
- Michigan was the first state to guarantee the right to tax-paid high school education.
- Grand Rapids was the first city in the United States to put fluoride in its water supply.
- The country's first regularly scheduled air-passenger service began operation between Grand Rapids and Detroit in 1926.
- In 1879 Detroit telephone customers were first in the nation to be assigned phone numbers.
- The Michigan State Police established the first state police radio system in the world in 1929.

The Written Word

William Austin Burt of Mount Vernon was the first to receive a patent for his "typographer"— the first typewriter. Burt's invention was used on May 25, 1829, by John P. Sheldon, editor of Detroit's *Michigan Gazette.* He sent the first-ever typewritten letter to then-secretary of state Martin Van Buren.

Traffic Lines

The road commissioner of Wayne County had a brainstorm — paint lines on the road to indicate where cars should drive. In the fall of 1911, River Road, near Trenton, was the first road to be painted with a dividing stripe. At the time the lines were

white and painted by hand. Later, machines were developed that painted the lines automatically.

Two Lands in One

> ... the Prospect is terminated with some Hills covered with Vineyards, Trees bearing good Fruit, Groves, and Forests, so well dispos'd, that one would think Nature alone could not have made, without the Help of Art, so charming a Prospect.
>
> — *Louis Hennepin, 1679*

The earliest inhabitants of Michigan arrived sometime around 9000 B.C. Little is known except that they hunted with flint arrowheads. Around 5000 B.C. they began using copper to make tools, putting them among the first people in the Western Hemisphere to work with metal. Native peoples also developed ceramic pottery, began burying their tribal members in burial mounds, and — around A.D. 100 — began developing agriculture.

In the early 1600s, when the first Europeans arrived, several Native tribes lived in the area. All of these tribes spoke variants of the same language, called Algonquian.

The Ottawas were traders who lived primarily in northern Michigan. Their canoes traveled as far west as Green Bay, Wisconsin, and as far east as Quebec to buy and sell cornmeal, furs, sunflower oil, tobacco, and medicinal herbs. The Ottawa lived in agricultural villages in summer and separated into family groups for winter hunts.

The Ojibwa people lived in Michigan's Upper Peninsula in the early 1600s but moved west as the fur trade expanded. Each Ojibwa tribe was divided into migratory groups. In autumn these groups separated into families, and, in summer, groups gathered together, usually at fishing sites. A few groups cultivated corn. The Ojibwa also relied on the collection of wild rice. They made canoes, wigwams, and utensils out of birch tree bark.

The Menominee lived along the Menominee River, now part of the boundary between Wisconsin and Michigan's Upper Peninsula. Like the Ojibwa, the Menominee had

Native Americans of Michigan

Native Americans of Michigan
Huron
Iroquois Confederacy
Menominee
Ojibwa (Chippewa)
Ottawa
Potawatomi

DID YOU KNOW?

The French word for narrow is *detroit*. French explorers used the word to describe the point where Lake St. Clair passes into Lake Erie, and that is how Detroit, which was founded on that spot, got its name. If the explorers had been English, the city might now be known as Narrow, Michigan.

dome-shaped houses and lived by gathering wild rice and farming corn, squash, beans, and tobacco.

▲ An engraving by William James Bennett — Detroit as it was in 1836.

The First Europeans

Frenchman Étienne Brûlé was the first recorded European to explore what is now the Canadian province of Ontario. Samuel de Champlain, the leader of the French colony of New France, assigned Brûlé to learn more about the land and peoples to the west of the new city of Québec and to find out if the waters that emptied into the St. Lawrence River might be part of a waterway that reached the Pacific Ocean.

With de Champlain, Brûlé discovered Lake Ontario and probably reached Lake Superior. His maps were the first to show the St. Marys Falls that would be a barrier to the free flow of water traffic between Lake Huron and Lake

DID YOU KNOW?

The name *Michigan* comes from the Ojibwa word *michigama*, which means "great water."

Superior for another three hundred years. The details of Brûlé's death in 1633 are unknown, but according to several accounts, he was killed by the Hurons.

In early 1634, de Champlain sent Jean Nicolet to continue Brûlé's work. Nicolet had lived with a tribe on Allumette Island in the Ottawa River in order to learn the Algonquian language and culture. Nicolet canoed through the Straits of Mackinac and along the Lake Michigan shore of Michigan's Upper Peninsula. He believed that he would find the Orient if he canoed far enough west, but the waters took him only as far west as Green Bay, Wisconsin.

Mission Accomplished

As early as 1614 Catholic missionaries had settled among the Hurons, trying to convert them to Catholicism and the European way of life. By the 1630s this work had come under the control of the Jesuits, and in 1641, two Jesuit priests, Isaac Jogues and Charles Raymbault, retraced Brûlé's route of two decades earlier. The two conducted the first Christian services in Michigan for a crowd of about two thousand Ojibwa at what is now Sault Ste. Marie.

The Jesuits were interested in spreading Catholicism, but French colonial authorities were interested in spreading loyalty to the French Empire. So, in addition to giving sermons, the Jesuits also gave speeches meant to impress

Forced Out

The influx of European settlers forced many Native tribes to migrate both west and north. Among the tribes who migrated to Michigan were:

The Huron, originally from Ohio and New York, were later forced out of Michigan and moved west to Kansas and then to Oklahoma.

The Miami, from the Green Bay area of Wisconsin, had also been native to Ohio. They later moved to Indiana.

▼ Sault Ste. Marie today.

the Native tribes with France's power. In 1671 the Jesuits gave a speech to a large crowd, and afterward, a French official laid formal claim to the lands of Michigan.

Two years later Frenchmen Father Jacques Marquette and Louis Jolliet journeyed along the northern shores of Lake Michigan, into Green Bay, and from there down Wisconsin's rivers to the Mississippi to the point where it joins the waters of the Arkansas River. This was one of the greatest exploratory voyages of the time and provided the first accurate description of the river's course.

The Fur Trade

The fur trade played an important role in the seventeenth century. Michigan tribes, including the Huron, acted as middlemen, taking furs from Great Lakes tribes down to trading posts on the St. Lawrence River and returning with trade goods. In the 1640s the Iroquois attacked the Huron because they wanted to take over the middleman role, especially in trading with the Dutch in the Hudson Valley.

Since the Huron had worked closely with the French, the French became nervous when the Iroquois forced the Huron out of the area. They were afraid that the Iroquois had been backed by another European power — the English or the Dutch. French traders moved into the Great Lakes region to protect their fur interests.

By the 1670s hundreds of fur traders and their employees, called *voyageurs,* were arriving every year. Missions such as those at Sault Ste. Marie and St. Ignace became convenient bases for trade.

Father Jacques Marquette
1637–1675

In the late 1600s Father Jacques Marquette of France arrived to establish a mission at Sault Ste. Marie, intending to convert the local Ojibwa. The small chapel and house that he built, enclosed within a wooden stockade fence, was the first European settlement in Michigan.

Although it was abandoned after thirty years, its location was ideal — on the river linking the largest of the Great Lakes — and it was settled again by the French later in the 1700s. Meanwhile, Marquette established a second mission in 1671 on the north side of the Straits of Mackinac.

Today the city of St. Ignace stands where his second mission used to be. A statue commemorating Father Marquette stands on the island of Mackinac, which is located in the strait between Lake Michigan and Lake Huron.

In the 1680s the Iroquois tried to terrorize the Great Lakes tribes into trading with them. Their trading partners, the English, came as far west as the Straits of Mackinac. The French acted quickly by building forts in Michigan for the first time. As a result of the increased French presence, the fur trade increased wildly. By 1696 so many furs were flowing into France that prices dropped and the furs were practically worthless. King Louis XIV ordered all French traders to withdraw from the trading posts, except for one in Illinois. By 1698 the French soldiers, fur traders, and Jesuits were gone.

A few years later, however, Louis XIV decided he didn't want the English to expand their colonies. He authorized the return of French soldiers, and strongholds were established as far south as New Orleans and as far north as the narrow waterway connecting Lake Huron and Lake Erie.

In 1701 Antoine de la Mothe Cadillac established Detroit as a fur-trading center and administrative post. It soon became the leading French community in the entire Great Lakes area. Detroit was also the first permanent European settlement in Michigan, and it was settled by both French people and Native Americans.

▼ A re-creation of a fur trader's cabin.

The French and Indian War

By 1750 English settlers in the Atlantic colonies were seeking more farmland. The French had claimed the lands west of the Appalachians, but several English colonies claimed their royal charters gave them the rights to parts of these same lands. The French were determined to keep the English out, and the English were determined to move in. In 1754 the struggle over land set off the final colonial conflict in North America between Great Britain and France. The English colonists called the conflict the French and Indian War because the French and various Native American tribes stood in the way of English expansion to the west.

No combat took place in Michigan, but Michigan Native Americans fought the English under the leadership of Frenchman Charles Langlade. In 1755 Langlade and his warriors ambushed and routed British forces led by General Edward Braddock, the greatest French victory in the war. Eventually, however, the British prevailed. In 1760 the governor of New France surrendered the remaining lands to the west, including Michigan. In the 1763 Treaty of Paris, Britain acquired rule over Canada and the French Empire east of the Mississippi, except for New Orleans. However, many French settlers remained in the area, and until the 1820s, the majority of Michigan's non-Native population had French ancestry.

▲ During the French and Indian War, General Edward Braddock (shown above) had under his command a young field officer named George Washington.

Michigan Territory

During the American Revolution a force of Spanish soldiers from St. Louis moved into Michigan and in 1781 occupied Fort St. Joseph in southwestern Michigan for twenty-four hours before returning to St. Louis. As a result of this brief conquest, Spain claimed it was entitled to territory east of the Mississippi. The British, however, ceded to the Americans everything east of the Mississippi in the 1783 treaty recognizing American independence. In 1787 Michigan became part of the newly created Northwest Territory. The British still kept some soldiers in Detroit and other major Michigan posts until 1796.

In 1800, Michigan was split between the Northwest and Indiana Territories. All of it then became part of Indiana Territory before it was established as the Territory of Michigan in 1805. During the War of 1812, Michigan's first governor, William Hull, surrendered Detroit to the British — but in 1813 the land became U.S. territory again, thanks to the victory of Commodore Oliver Hazard Perry at the Battle of Lake Erie.

The real growth of the Michigan Territory began after the war ended, when new governor Lewis Cass encouraged settlement. The development of the steamship, which linked Detroit with Buffalo, New York, inaugurated a new era in lake transportation. The Erie Canal's completion in 1825 made Detroit a leading distribution point for settlers from the East who sought new homes.

Statehood and Growth

Michigan's first constitution was enacted in 1835, but statehood was delayed until 1837 after a boundary dispute with Ohio, called the "Toledo War," was settled.

The state grew rapidly. Thousands of agricultural settlers arrived, and Detroit and other cities profited from the influx of people. In the 1840s people discovered that the Upper Peninsula had rich iron and copper resources. The state capital was moved from Detroit to the more central location of Lansing in 1847.

▼ In this painting depicting the Battle of Lake Erie, Commodore Oliver H. Perry is rowed to the ship *Niagra* after his flagship, the *Lafayette,* is destroyed.

Michigan had entered the Union as a free state, and slavery had ended there by 1830. Throughout the U.S. Civil War, Michigan made major contributions to the Union cause. A black regiment from Michigan included enlistees from many states and from Ontario.

A meeting of antislavery northerners in Wisconsin, in 1854, is commonly believed to be the first meeting of the Republican Party. At about the same time, however, another group of antislavery activists met in Michigan to form a political party. They, too, called themselves Republicans.

The Twentieth Century

Before 1900 all of Michigan's counties had been settled. The major industries were farming, lumber, mining, and manufacturing. Michigan factories manufactured chemicals such as soda ash and bromine; the Dow Chemical Company was incorporated there in 1897. Other factories manufactured shingles, cement, and pharmaceuticals. The economic landscape of Michigan — and the world — changed when the modern automotive industry developed.

During World War I industrial production at all levels was intensified, which benefited Michigan because of its many factories. However, the Great Depression was very severe in Michigan, since its industrial products (cars among them) were not necessities. Unemployment was far above the national average. In the 1930s automobile workers banded together in unions, which became powerful political forces in Michigan. In 1936-37 workers at General Motors' Flint plant engaged in a sit-down strike after GM fired several union men; the strike lasted for forty-four days.

Since World War II Michigan has had ups and downs. Racial tensions came to a head in the Detroit riots of 1943 and 1967. On the other hand the state has also made strong efforts to equalize opportunity for minorities, women, and people with disabilities.

During the postwar years the development of suburbs and the U.S. highway system led to an increased demand for cars, which boosted the Michigan economy. More recently, however, international competition and other factors have led to economic downturns for the automotive industry, which have had a profound effect on Michigan.

Driving the Economy

In 1896 three men experimented in Michigan with "horseless carriages:" Charles King, Henry Ford, and Ransom Olds *(pictured left)*. All three used gasoline engines, and at first, Olds was most successful. By the early 1900s, though, Ford established himself by applying mass-production techniques to the assembly of his Model T, bringing the car's cost down to a point where most people could afford it. In the 1920s Ford's position slipped, and the leading auto producer became General Motors, run by Billy Durant. Durant knew very little about how to invent cars, but he knew how to run a business. By the end of the 1920s, the Michigan-based Big Three — General Motors, Ford, and Chrysler — produced 75 percent of the nation's cars; automobiles assumed the dominant position in Michigan's economy.

Making It in Michigan

> I have found that every man's success or failure in life is bounded on the North by the top of his head, on the East and West by his ears, and on the South by the back of his neck; and I have also learned that we get those things in this life that we think about the most and strive for the hardest.
>
> — *W. L. Brownell*, It's Up to Me, *1908*

Today Michiganders can claim almost every ancestry imaginable. Michigan has seen waves of immigrants from Poland and Italy, and the Upper Peninsula has a large Finnish population. Many Michigan families come from Cornwall, England, while western Michigan was settled by Dutch immigrants. Germans settled throughout the state, and Irish people settled primarily in urban areas.

Many of the state's ethnic communities live in particular areas. One reason for this voluntary segregation might be the many lakes and waterways in the state, which divided it neatly into regions where different communities settled.

In addition to being culturally diverse, Michigan is also racially diverse. The most significant population change in

Age Distribution in Michigan

0–4	672,005
5–19	2,212,060
20–24	643,839
25–44	2,960,544
45–64	2,230,978
65 and over	1,219,018

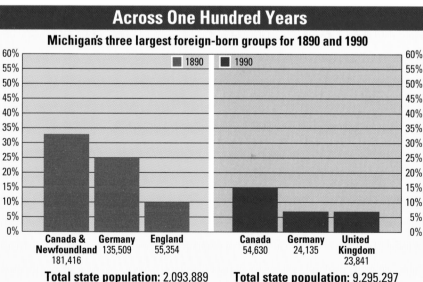

Across One Hundred Years
Michigan's three largest foreign-born groups for 1890 and 1990

1890 / 1990

Canada & Newfoundland 181,416 — Germany 135,509 — England 55,354
Canada 54,630 — Germany 24,135 — United Kingdom 23,841

Total state population: 2,093,889
Total foreign-born: 543,160 (26%)

Total state population: 9,295,297
Total foreign-born: 353,993 (4%)

Patterns of Immigration

The total number of people who immigrated to Michigan in 1998 was 13,943. Of that number, the largest immigrant groups were from India (11%), the Dominican Republic (8%), and Mexico (8%).

the 1900s was the growth of the African-American community, from fewer than sixteen thousand in 1900 to more than 1.4 million a century later. More than 50 percent of Michigan's African-American population lives in Detroit.

▲ The Renaissance Center in Detroit.

Where Michiganders Live

Seventy percent of Michiganders live in urban areas, with the Detroit metropolitan area representing over half of the

Heritage and Background, Michigan   Year 2000

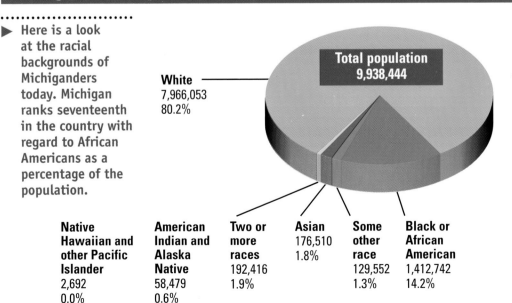

▶ Here is a look at the racial backgrounds of Michiganders today. Michigan ranks seventeenth in the country with regard to African Americans as a percentage of the population.

Total population 9,938,444

White
7,966,053
80.2%

Note: 3.3% (323,877) of the population identify themselves as **Hispanic** or **Latino,** a cultural designation that crosses racial lines. Hispanics and Latinos are counted in this category and the racial category of their choice.

Native Hawaiian and other Pacific Islander
2,692
0.0%

American Indian and Alaska Native
58,479
0.6%

Two or more races
192,416
1.9%

Asian
176,510
1.8%

Some other race
129,552
1.3%

Black or African American
1,412,742
14.2%

state's total population. These overall percentages remain true even though all of Michigan's major cities have decreased in population over the last few decades. Between 1990 and 2000, for instance, Detroit's population decreased by 7.5 percent, and Flint's population decreased by just over 11 percent.

In the late 1990s a new population shift began. Now Michigan's towns of fewer than twenty-five hundred people are growing more quickly than its cities.

Still, most Michiganders remain in large urban areas; most of these people live in the southern part of the Lower Peninsula. Detroit remains the state's largest city and the nation's tenth largest. Including its nearby suburbs, it is the eighth largest metropolitan area in the United States.

Today Michigan's population includes more than forty national and ethnic groups. Its largest distinct population group comes from across the border, in Canada. The next largest is African American; after that comes Asian, then Native American (which includes members of Michigan's

Educational Levels of Michigan Workers	
Less than 9th grade	452,893
9th to 12th grade, no diploma	903,866
High school graduate	1,887,449
Some college, no degree	1,191,518
Associate degree	392,869
Bachelor's degree	638,267
Graduate or professional degree	375,780

▼ The skyline of Detroit, Michigan's most populous city.

Native tribes as well as Inuit people and Aleutian Islanders), followed by Latinos and Asian/Pacific Islanders.

The largest portion of Michigan's current Native American population is Ojibwa. By the 1900s about thirty thousand members of the tribe (most of mixed ancestry) lived on reservations in several states, including Michigan.

About 29 percent of the population over the age of three is enrolled in school, making Michigan tenth in the nation in school enrollment. About 7 percent of those over twenty-five have finished only elementary school and junior high; 76.8 percent of Michiganders over twenty-five have finished high school, and 17.4 percent of the over-twenty-five population has attained college degrees.

Religion

The first European settlers in Michigan were French Catholics. Thereafter, the state attracted many Catholic immigrants from other countries such as Ireland, Italy, and Poland. As of 1990, 23 percent of those Michiganders who claimed a religious affiliation were Catholic. Many of the people who settled Michigan in the nineteenth century were Protestants from Germany, known as Lutherans. There are still nearly five hundred thousand Lutherans in the state.

Other Protestant groups include Methodists, Presbyterians, Pentecostals, Congregationalists, and Episcopalians. These are just a few of the almost two hundred Protestant denominations in the state. Baptists are the largest group of Protestants in the state, making up 15 percent of the state's total population of religiously affiliated Michiganders.

Religious diversity is most apparent in Detroit, where the state's first synagogue was built in 1851. Orthodox, Conservative, Reformed, and Hasidic Jews make up 0.3 percent of the state's population. Detroit is home to about two thousand Muslims and at least twelve mosques and Islamic centers. The proportion of Michiganders who are Hindu is exactly that of the United States — 0.2 percent. There are at least three Buddhist temples in Michigan to serve the 0.1 percent of Michiganders who identify themselves as Buddhists.

▲ Lots of snow means Michiganders learn to ski young.

The Great Lakes State

> The beautiful and fertile lands of the lower peninsula, now studded with happy homes and flourishing cities, and traversed in every direction by the locomotive, were traversed only by wild beasts, and wilder men.
>
> — *Charles Richard Tuttle, 1873*

Michigan is surprisingly large — the distance from Monroe in the southeast to Ironwood in the northwest is similar to the distance between Atlanta and Chicago.

Michigan's landscape includes white sand beaches on the Lake Michigan shore, forests, and quick-running rivers. The state's proximity to Lake Michigan and the other Great Lakes serves to temper the climate of Michigan, making it milder than the climate of other Midwestern states. Lake Michigan also divides the state into two segments — the Upper and Lower Peninsulas. Though the Upper Peninsula is cooler than the Lower, the difference in temperature range between far northern and far southern cities is not high.

Although the peninsulas are the easiest divisions to make, the state's geography points to a different split — between the Superior Upland, a rugged, mineral-rich area where elevations reach more than 1,900 feet (579 m), and the Central Lowland, a mildly rolling area with sandy soil.

DID YOU KNOW?

Although Michigan is nicknamed "The Wolverine State," wolverines have never lived in Michigan. Early Native traders brought wolverine pelts from Canada to trade with the French, and for some reason the nickname stuck.

▼ *From left to right:* **Detroit; Sleeping Bear Dunes; Tahquamenon Falls; Old Mill Creek Historic Park; Pictured Rocks; Tahquamenon Falls in winter.**

Upland and Lowland

The Upland is found in the western region of the Upper Peninsula, where the abundance of copper and iron ore once made the area economically dependent on mining. Ironwood, Iron Mountain, Hancock, Houghton, and Marquette are among the larger cities. Tourism and recreation offer possibilities for diversifying the economy.

The eastern counties of the Upper Peninsula and the Lower Peninsula make up the northern Michigan portion of the Central Lowland. White pine forests once grew here. Although most of the old trees were chopped down, some trees north of Grayling are three hundred years old and stand over 150 feet (46 m) tall.

The sandy soil, with adequate moisture, produces an abundant yield of potatoes and grain. Fruit grows along the Lake Michigan shore because the lake's influence prevents early killing frosts. (Large bodies of water, such as the Great Lakes, make weather less extreme; summers are slightly cooler and winters slightly warmer.)

The towns in the north serve as regional centers for tourists and farmers and often as headquarters for governmental services. Many of the larger communities have attracted small-scale manufacturing. Northern Michigan's cities include Sault Ste. Marie, Petoskey, Ludington, Manistee, Cadillac, and Traverse City.

South of Bay City and Muskegon, a fertile clay soil and a longer growing season permit a wider variety of crops, especially grains. Bog soils, created as ancient lakes slowly became filled with organic matter, exist throughout the state, especially in the southeastern Lower Peninsula. These soils are ideal for growing vegetables.

The southern counties produce much of the state's agricultural wealth. The region also contains many

The Soo Canals

The Soo Canals located in Sault Ste. Marie permit ships to pass between Lakes Superior and Huron. Ships traveling east carry about 90 percent of the cargo passing through the canals; most of the cargo is iron ore, grain, and coal. About eighty-five million tons of cargo pass through these canals each year. The St. Marys River connects these two lakes, but there are strong rapids in the river, and most early trappers carried their canoes and furs around the rough water rather than risk "running" the rapids.

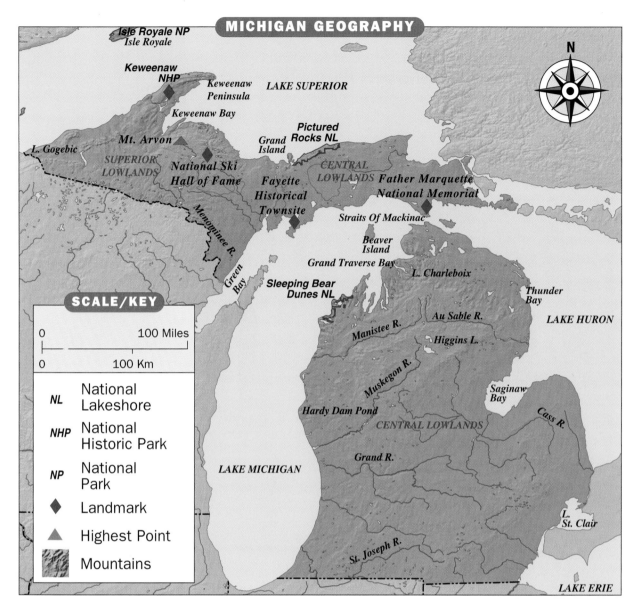

SCALE/KEY

0	100 Miles
0	100 Km

NL — National Lakeshore

NHP — National Historic Park

NP — National Park

◆ — Landmark

▲ — Highest Point

▨ — Mountains

Map labels: Isle Royale NP, Isle Royale, Keweenaw NHP, Keweenaw Peninsula, Keweenaw Bay, LAKE SUPERIOR, Pictured Rocks NL, Grand Island, L. Gogebic, Mt. Arvon, SUPERIOR LOWLANDS, National Ski Hall of Fame, CENTRAL LOWLANDS, Fayette Historical Townsite, Father Marquette National Memorial, Menominee R., Straits Of Mackinac, Beaver Island, Green Bay, Grand Traverse Bay, L. Charleboix, Thunder Bay, Sleeping Bear Dunes NL, LAKE HURON, Au Sable R., Manistee R., Higgins L., Muskegon R., Saginaw Bay, Cass R., Hardy Dam Pond, CENTRAL LOWLANDS, LAKE MICHIGAN, Grand R., L. St. Clair, St. Joseph R., LAKE ERIE

factories and several large cities, including Detroit, Flint, Lansing, Grand Rapids, and Battle Creek.

Climate

In July, the average temperature in Sault Ste. Marie is 64° Fahrenheit (18° Celsius); in Detroit, 73°F (23°C). The corresponding January averages are 14°F (-10°C) and 26°F (-3°C). Southern Michigan is the wettest part of the state; the average annual precipitation for the entire state is 31 inches (79 centimeters). The coastal strip along Lake Michigan receives an unusually large snowfall from westerly storms moving across the lake.

▼ A Canadian goose at the Kellogg Bird Sanctuary in Augusta.

Wildlife

Most of Michigan was once heavily wooded. Genuine prairies were found only in the southwestern part of the state. Most forests held hardwood trees such as ash, oak, and hemlock. In the north, white and Norway pine were commonly found.

Although much of Michigan's original forest has been chopped down, the state began replacing forests in 1903, planting millions of white spruce trees, as well as red and white jack pines.

Many animals are native to Michigan. Over 350 bird species live in the state or migrate through it. The state was the first in the country to establish a network of protected "rest stops" for migrating Canada geese.

Whitefish, lake trout, and salmon swim in the Great Lakes, and many of Michigan's streams contain trout, walleye, and northern pike. In the inland lakes there are perch, pike, and bass. Many fur-bearing mammals, such as beavers, were sought eagerly by early traders and live in Michigan to this day. Deer and bears, as well as quail and ducks, remain numerous in many counties.

Lakes and Rivers

Michigan is home to many rivers, most of which are in the southern part of the Lower Peninsula. These rivers are generally shallow and narrow. Relatively easy to navigate and bridge, they encouraged settlement as Michigan's "highways" before paved roads and motorized transportation. Several rivers, especially in the Upper Peninsula, have waterfalls that are now used for generating power.

There are eleven thousand lakes in Michigan that range in size from a few acres to thousands. Michigan is also surrounded by Great Lakes, which some call "America's Inland Seas." The four Great Lakes that border Michigan are Lake Michigan, Lake Superior, Lake Erie, and Lake Huron.

About five hundred islands dot Michigan's lakes and rivers. Some of the islands are wild; others, like Grosse Isle, are residential. On Mackinac Island motor vehicles are prohibited. A virgin wilderness of nearly 900 square miles (2,331 sq km), Isle Royale is a national park in western Lake Superior.

High Points
Mt. Arvon
1,979 feet (603 m)

Average January temperature range
Lansing: 22.5°F (-5.3°C)
Detroit: 25.5°F (-3.6 °C)

Average July temperature range
Lansing: 70.9°F
 (21.6°C)
Detroit: 73.2°F (22.9°C)

Average yearly rainfall
Lansing: 29 inches
 (74 cm)
Detroit: 32.4 inches
 (82 cm)

Average yearly snowfall
Lansing: 49 inches
 (124 cm)
Detroit: 42 in (107 cm)

Largest Lakes

Lake Superior
383 miles (616 km) long
160 miles (258 km)
 wide at widest point

Lake Michigan
321 miles (517 km) long
118 miles (190 km)
 wide at widest point

Lake Erie
241 miles (388 km) long
57 miles (91.7 km) wide
 at widest point

Lake Huron
206 miles (331 km) long
183 miles (295 km)
 wide at widest point

The Car Capital of the World

> What's good for General Motors is good
> for the country.
>
> — *Charles Wilson, president of General Motors, 1953*

The shift from hunting and trapping to agriculture was a strong part of Michigan's colonization by European and U.S. settlers. Agriculture remains important today. Grains are grown in the south, potatoes in the north. Fruit is grown along the coastal strip of Lake Michigan, where the climate is more moderate.

Mining has been one of Michigan's traditional strengths, especially in the iron and copper rich Upper Peninsula, although the importance of this industry has declined.

Michigan also produces metals, food products, and chemicals. There are many paper-recycling plants in the UP, which recycle almost every kind of paper into reusable materials. Michigan is also home to food factories, including Kellogg and Post cereal makers and Gerber Baby Foods.

Because of the beauty of its landscape, especially around the Great Lakes, tourism is another positive economic force in Michigan. Tourism brings Michigan millions of dollars each year, giving the state an incentive to protect forests, rivers, lakes, and shorelines from development and pollution.

Automobile Ups and Downs

Michigan depends on its automobile manufacturing, and the state's economy is tied to the automobile industry. In the late 1970s oil prices rose sharply, imported cars became cheaper and were more fuel-efficient than U.S. cars, and the nation was in an economic recession. These factors combined to cause an economic crisis in Michigan.

Between 1979 and 1982 the state's unemployment level climbed above 15 percent, the highest in the nation. Since then the auto industry has made a modest comeback, and Michigan's government and business leaders have initiated

Top Employers (of workers age sixteen and over)	
Services	31.0%
Retail and wholesale trade	21.0%
Manufacturing	19.0%
Government	12.0%
Finance, insurance, and real estate	5.0%
Construction	4.9%
Agriculture	1.0%
Mining	0.2%

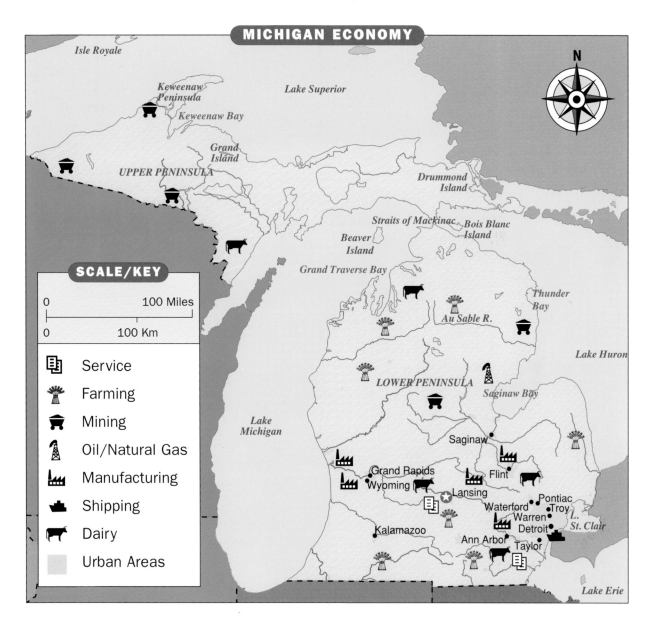

MICHIGAN ECONOMY

SCALE/KEY

0 — 100 Miles
0 — 100 Km

- 📰 Service
- 🌾 Farming
- ⛏ Mining
- 🛢 Oil/Natural Gas
- 🏭 Manufacturing
- 🚢 Shipping
- 🐄 Dairy
- Urban Areas

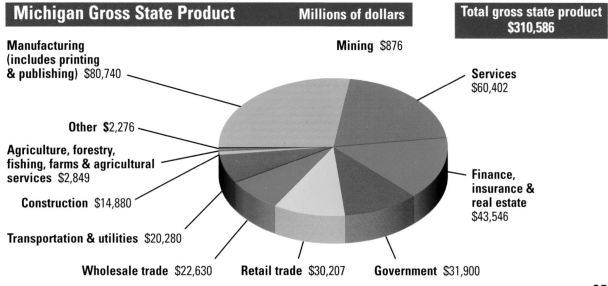

Michigan Gross State Product

Millions of dollars

Total gross state product $310,586

Manufacturing (includes printing & publishing) $80,740

Mining $876

Services $60,402

Other $2,276

Agriculture, forestry, fishing, farms & agricultural services $2,849

Construction $14,880

Transportation & utilities $20,280

Finance, insurance & real estate $43,546

Wholesale trade $22,630

Retail trade $30,207

Government $31,900

programs to expand the state's manufacturing base. However, the automotive industry continues to dominate the economy, accounting for about one-third of all manufacturing employment.

▲ *Above:* Cars being manufactured.
At left: One of Kellogg's "grrreat" products.

In 1994 Michigan's unemployment rate fell below the national average for the first time in thirty years. Michigan's share of U.S. auto production increased to 24 percent in 1999, after steadily declining each year since 1995.

Union Action 1936–1937

Auto factories were tough places to work during the industry's early years. The pace of work was controlled by the ever-increasing speed of the assembly line, and the foreman held the power to hire or fire workers at will. Many jobs were physically demanding, machines had few safety devices, and industrial accidents were common. On August 26, 1935, auto workers organized the United Auto Workers union (UAW) to bargain for better wages and better working conditions.

On December 30, 1936, UAW leaders decided to call

Made in Michigan

Leading farm products and crops
Dairy products (milk and cream)
Soybeans
Sugar beets
Dry beans
Cattle
Hogs
Eggs

Other products
Transportation equipment
Industrial machinery and equipment
Fabricated metal products
Furniture and fixtures
Electronic and electrical machinery

a strike against General Motors (GM). The goal of the strike was simple — GM recognition of the UAW. For more than six weeks, members of the UAW stopped production and refused to leave the plants. They slept on unfinished car seats, eating food their families and friends slipped through factory windows. They faced tear gas attacks and heat shutoffs and battled with police and company security guards. Michigan Governor Frank Murphy sent in the National Guard to maintain order.

Faced with an enormous loss of production, GM conceded to the strikers' demands and signed a one-page document agreeing to bargain with the UAW. The strike shaped the future not only of Michigan, and not only of automobile workers, but also of laborers around the country.

▲ Michigan is the United States' leading grower of tart cherries, producing from 70 to 75 percent of the nation's crop each year. Tart cherries are used mostly in pies, preserves, jellies, juices, and other products. Michigan is also usually the United States' fourth largest producer of sweet cherries, producing about 20 percent of the nation's crop most years. Sweet cherries are often eaten fresh, although they are sometimes canned or frozen.

Natural Resources

Michigan once mined a great deal of copper and iron ore, and the state is still one of the nation's leading producers of iron ore. However, changes in the U.S. steel industry have made mining ore less profitable than it used to be, and by 1984 most mining activities in Michigan's Menominee Range had ceased.

Michigan also has land resources, which are used by farmers and foresters to make a living. Although fewer people farm each year, Michigan is still a major agricultural state because of its fertile soil. Corn is Michigan's major field crop, but the state is best known for its production of cucumbers and fruit. Michigan leads the nation in the production of cherries and blueberries; the state is also a major producer of apples. Most years the state is also the leading producer of dry beans in the United States.

Christmas trees are another important agricultural product. Michigan forests also produce large quantities of pulpwood products, and the timber industry there is undergoing a revival.

International Airports

Airport	Location	Passengers per Year (2000)
Detroit Metropolitan Wayne County International	Detroit	35,535,080
Gerald R. Ford International	Grand Rapids	1,905,357

DID YOU KNOW?

The first railroad in Michigan, the Erie and Kalamazoo, was completed between Toledo and Adrian in 1836.

Government for the People

> As we seek the American Dream, as we build the Next Michigan, our shared virtues and our civic responsibilities remain the rock upon which we stand — together.
>
> — *Michigan Governor John Engler, in his speech "Building the Next Michigan," January 2001*

When Michigan began to move toward statehood in the mid-1800s, there was an obstacle in its path. Michigan was engaged in a boundary dispute with its neighbor state, Ohio, over a piece of land called "The Toledo Strip." Until that dispute was settled, President Andrew Jackson refused to sign the bill granting Michigan entry into the Union. The dispute was settled in Ohio's favor, but Michigan received the Upper Peninsula as compensation. It was a near thing, however — the first convention held to approve the land compromise, on September 26, 1836, rejected it. On October 29 a new convention was assembled and the compromise passed. When the news was conveyed to Washington, D.C., Congress approved the bill, and on January 26, 1837, President Jackson signed it.

Still, Michigan did not have its request for statehood automatically granted. In the years following the Compromise of 1820, the federal government would only grant statehood if both a "free" and a "slave" state were admitted to the Union at the same time. Luckily for Michigan, at that time Arkansas also entered the Union as a slave state.

Michigan's Constitutional Convention had been held in 1835, and the state has had five constitutional conventions since then. The most recent and abiding constitution was adopted on April 1, 1963.

Michigan State Constitution

We, the PEOPLE of the territory of Michigan . . . believing that the time has arrived when our present political condition ought to cease, and the right of self-government be asserted . . . do, by our delegates in convention assembled, mutually agree to form ourselves into a free and independent state, by the style and title of "The State of Michigan," and do ordain and establish the following constitution for the government of the same.

Preamble to the First Michigan State Constitution

Like the U.S. government, Michigan's government is divided into three branches — executive, legislative, and judicial.

The Executive Branch

The executive branch is led by the governor, who serves for four years and, with a lieutenant governor, can only serve for two terms. The governor is responsible for most important governmental services. The governor must appoint administrative commissions that are responsible for overseeing various departments within the state.

Regardless of the governor's political affiliation, some of the departments must be bipartisan (made up of members

Elected Posts in the Executive Branch		
Office	**Length of Term**	**Term Limits**
Governor	4 years	Two terms
Lieutenant Governor	4 years	Two terms
Secretary of State	4 years	Two terms
Attorney General	4 years	Two terms

▼ The Michigan State Capitol was completed in 1879.

of different political parties). This ensures that all Michigan's people are represented, regardless of the way they voted. The governor is also responsible for signing bills into law and is given fourteen days to sign or veto each bill. If, within these fourteen days, the governor neither signs nor vetoes the bill, it becomes law. If, however, the legislature adjourns for the year before those fourteen days are up, the unsigned bill does not become law.

Other members of Michigan's executive branch are the attorney general, secretary of state, and sixteen cabinet heads.

The Legislative Branch

The legislative branch, also known as the General Assembly, is *bicameral* — which means it has two legislative chambers. They are the Senate and the House of Representatives. There are thirty-eight senators, each elected for four-year terms. Like the members of the executive branch of government, senators can serve a maximum of two terms. The House of Representatives has 110 members elected for two-year terms. Representatives are allowed to serve for three terms. The job of the legislature is to make laws for the people of Michigan.

A bill for a new law must pass in both houses before it can be sent to the governor to be signed into law. Either the Senate or the House can originate a bill. If, however, either house makes changes to a bill it is presented with, then the house that originally proposed the bill must approve it again. A simple majority in each house is required to approve a bill.

If a bill is vetoed by the governor, the General Assembly can call another vote on the bill. To override the governor's veto, the bill needs to pass with at least a two-thirds majority in both houses.

General Assembly			
House	Number of Members	Length of Term	Term Limits
Senate	38 senators	4 years	2 terms
House of Representatives	110 representatives	2 years	3 terms

The Judicial Branch

The judicial branch is made up of several courts at different levels. The highest court in the judicial branch is the seven-

GERALD FORD Born in 1913, Gerald Ford is the only U.S. vice president to become president upon the resignation of a chief executive. President Richard M. Nixon resigned  on August 9, 1974, and Ford took office that same day. Ford, a longtime Republican congressman from Michigan, had been vice president for only eight months. Nixon had appointed him to succeed Vice President Spiro T. Agnew, who resigned in a corruption scandal. Ford's popularity as president dropped when he pardoned Nixon for any crimes that Nixon might have committed while president. When Ford ran for election to a full term in 1976, he was defeated by Democrat Jimmy Carter.

member state supreme court. The chief justice and the six associate justices are elected for eight-year terms. Each justice is nominated by a political party, and voters decide in general elections. If there is a midterm vacancy, then the position is filled by a gubernatorial appointment. The state also has an eight-member court of appeals, fifty-seven circuit courts for conducting trials, probate courts to oversee wills and estates, and other courts that are specified by the legislature.

A Separate State?

Michigan is divided into eighty-three counties, each governed by an elected board of commissioners. Until the 1930s the Republican Party in Michigan dominated national, state, and local elections. Since then the state's political affiliations have been more evenly divided.

Unions have been very active in Michigan politics, and the United Automobile Workers has endorsed candidates at the municipal, state, and national levels.

Some people in the Upper Peninsula feel their interests and needs are different from those who live in the Lower Peninsula. Every few years UP lawmakers suggest that they form a separate state. They want to call their state "Superior."

So far, these efforts have not succeeded. Occasionally, UP lawmakers suggest that the UP should join with Wisconsin. They say that their rural, small-town lifestyle is more like that of northern Wisconsinites than that of the city dwellers in the southern part of their own state.

First African-American Mayor

Coleman Young, born in 1918, was elected the first African-American mayor of Detroit in 1973. He was reelected four times. During Young's first years in office, the Detroit economy (and the nation's) was in decline, which made his job harder. When the economy is bad, people often try to blame the lack of jobs on scapegoats, and both African Americans and whites wanted to blame each other for the economic hard times. Young worked hard to prevent divisiveness and is remembered for building biracial coalitions within the Democratic Party. He died in 1997, four years after stepping down from the mayor's post

Motown and More

> The society of Detroit is very choice; and, as it has continued so since the old colonial days, through the territorial days, there is every reason to think that it will become, under its new dignities, a more and more desirable place of residence.
>
> — *Harriet Martineau,* Society in America, *1837*

▼ The Kalamazoo Institute of Arts has been drawing students and art lovers since 1924.

Detroit is the cultural center of Michigan. It is home to a symphony orchestra and the Detroit Institute of Arts. Like many cities, Detroit became a cultural center because its multicultural population created a cosmopolitan atmosphere in which the arts could flourish and grow. Michigan's first traveling theatrical companies performed in Detroit, and an opera house was erected there before the Civil War.

Woods and water dominate Michigan's landscape. Outside of Detroit and other major metropolitan centers, they provide opportunities for recreation. People have been vacationing in Michigan's forest and lake areas since the 1830s. Today many people go there to swim, fish, hike, and hunt — and, in the winter, to ice skate and cross-country ski.

Today Michigan has more than ninety state-operated parks and recreation areas. In addition Michigan's 3,900,000 acres (1,578,330 hectares) of state forest and 25,000,000 acres (10,116,951 ha) of national forest make up the largest

range of publicly owned forestland in any state east of the Rocky Mountains.

Community Fairs

In Michigan's rural areas, community-related arts have long held a central role. In pioneer days these were community harvest dances and county fairs. Today the traditions often take the form of community ethnic festivals, such as Holland's Tulip Time Festival and Frankenmuth's Bavarian Festival. While these celebrations each stem from a particular culture, they appeal to a wide range of Michiganders and tourists.

Other community fairs are based around themes, not ethnicities. These include northern lumbering festivals for Paul Bunyan Days, the National Cherry Festival in Traverse City, the annual Goose Festival in Fennville (celebrating the return of the Canada geese) and more.

Visual Art

Michigan is also home to several museums. The Detroit Institute of Arts, founded in 1885, holds one of the nation's

▲ The Frederick Meijer Botanical Gardens, in Grand Rapids, also include the da Vinci horse. The sculpture, *Il Cavallo*, was inspired by a sketch by Italian painter and sculptor Leonardo da Vinci. At 24 feet (7 m) high, it is the largest bronze horse sculpture in the world.

major collections. The Muskegon Museum of Art, founded in 1911, the Kalamazoo Institute of Arts, and the Grand Rapids Art Museum are also important parts of the Michigan cultural scene. Lansing is home to the Michigan Historical Museum, famous for its military and Native American collections, while many county museums commemorate local history.

Art isn't only found on the walls of museums, however. There are dozens of arts fairs held throughout the state. The Ann Arbor Art Fair — three fairs in one — is one of the biggest. Every year more than one-half million people attend Ann Arbor's Street Art Fair, Summer Art Fair, and State Street Art Fair to try to see as many of the more than one thousand booths as possible. World-class entertainment and food is also part of the fun.

Music

Michiganders enjoy every type of music, from rock to jazz to classical. The music for which Michigan is known best, however, came out of Detroit in the 1960s. It's called the "Motown Sound."

▼ Music mastermind Berry Gordy plays piano while some of the Motown's great voices, including Smokey Robinson and Stevie Wonder, sing along.

In the 1950s African Americans were singing a blend of gospel, rhythm and blues, and popular music. Since the record companies were owned by whites, very few black musicians got good recording deals. Berry Gordy Jr. changed this situation when he started a record company in 1959. He called his label Motown Records, short for Detroit's nickname Motor City. Within a year Motown had achieved its first gold record. The label skyrocketed many young singers to fame, including Diana Ross and the Supremes, the Temptations, the Four Tops, Stevie Wonder, Smokey Robinson, and the Jackson Five.

Colleges and Universities

There are more than one hundred colleges and universities in the state, including the University of Michigan, opened in 1837. There's a heated football rivalry between the University of Michigan and Michigan State University, which is the highlight of each season for many Michiganders.

▶ The lighthouse at Grand Haven is fondly known as "Big Red."

Lightkeeping

With four of the five Great Lakes lapping against Michigan's shores and 3,288 miles (5,291 km) of coastline, it's no wonder that lighthouses were needed — over 120. The first was erected in 1825, and its lighthouse beacons were fueled with whale oil and tended by lighthouse keepers. Today all of Michigan's working lighthouses are automated.

Michigan was the first state to establish a college of agriculture (Michigan State in East Lansing). It also opened the first teachers' college west of the Allegheny Mountains, Eastern Michigan University in Ypsilanti.

Northern Michigan University in Marquette is the only college in the nation that has a United States Olympic Education Center. The center is home to athletes training for the Olympics in events such as biathlon, cross-country skiing, luge, and short-track speed skating.

Sports

People have been playing organized team sports in Michigan since the late 1850s, when the first baseball teams were formed. In 1881 the Detroit team, the Tigers, began competing nationally. Other major teams in the Detroit area include the Lions, its National Football League team; the Red Wings, Detroit's

Sport	Team	Home
Baseball	Detroit Tigers	Comerica Park, Detroit
Basketball	Detroit Pistons	Palace of Auburn Hills, Auburn Hills
Women's Basketball	Detroit Shock	Palace of Auburn Hills, Auburn Hills
Football	Detroit Lions	Silverdome, Pontiac
Hockey	Detroit Red Wings	Joe Louis Arena, Detroit

▼ The Soo International 500 (I-500) is an annual snowmobile race held in Sault Ste. Marie.

National Hockey League team; and the Pistons, its National Basketball Association (NBA) team. Detroit is also home to the Women's National Basketball Association (WNBA) team the Detroit Shock.

The Tigers most recently won the World Series in 1984, the Pistons won the NBA championship in 1990, and the Red Wings took home the Stanley Cup in 1997. Fans are fiercely loyal, and the state's teams have given rise to several sports stars, including Ty Cobb, Joe Louis, and Lansing-born Earvin "Magic" Johnson, who once played college basketball for the Michigan State University Spartans.

◄ A 1912 baseball card featuring Hugh Jennings and Ty Cobb of the Detroit Tigers.

Great Michiganders

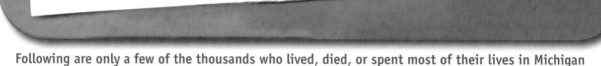

My Michigan! Thy progress shows
What loyal hearts can do . . .
— *"Michigan," lyrics by Marcus Peterson, 1894*

Following are only a few of the thousands who lived, died, or spent most of their lives in Michigan while making extraordinary contributions to the state and the nation.

CHIEF PONTIAC
STATESMAN

BORN: *circa 1720, on the Maumee River, OH*
DIED: *April 20, 1769, Cahokia, IL*

Pontiac was an Ottawa chief who became a great intertribal leader in 1763, when he organized resistance to the British in the Great Lakes area. During what was known as Pontiac's War, he attempted, unsuccessfully, to capture Detroit. Of the eleven other posts he attacked, his troops managed to seize eight. The British continued to resist, however, and by July 1766 Pontiac had agreed to a peace treaty.

SOJOURNER TRUTH
ABOLITIONIST

BORN: *1797, Ulster County, NY*
DIED: *November 26, 1883, Battle Creek*

A former slave born in New York, Isabella Van Wagener was freed by slaveholder Isaac Van Wagener just before New York State abolished slavery in 1827. With the help of Quaker friends, she recovered her son, who had been sold illegally into slavery in the South, and went to New York City. In 1843 she took the name Sojourner Truth. Leaving New York, she obeyed a personal calling "to travel up and down the land." At camp meetings, on street corners, and in churches she preached, sang, and debated, arguing for the rights of African Americans and women. In the 1850s she moved to Battle Creek, Michigan, and remained there until her death, supporting herself by selling copies of her book, *The Narrative of Sojourner Truth* (1850).

STEVENS T. MASON

PIONEER AND STATESMAN

BORN: *October 22, 1811, Stafford County, VA*
DIED: *January 4, 1843, New York, NY*

Born to an influential Virginia family, Mason came to Michigan as a young man when his father was appointed the secretary of Michigan and the family moved to Detroit. His father was unaccustomed to political life, and young Stevens became a savvy politician as he sought to protect his father from his detractors. By age nineteen, he was appointed acting territorial secretary and became acting territorial governor in 1834 at age twenty-two. He authorized a census, one of the requirements for statehood, and convened a constitutional convention. Michigan voters approved the constitution and elected Mason governor in 1835.

JOHN HARVEY KELLOGG

HEALTH FOOD ADVOCATE

BORN: *February 26, 1852, Tyrone*
DIED: *December 14, 1943, Battle Creek*

WILLIAM KEITH KELLOGG

HEALTH FOOD ADVOCATE

BORN: *April 7, 1860, Battle Creek*
DIED: *October 6, 1951, Battle Creek*

These brothers launched one of the nation's first health food kicks. A Seventh-Day Adventist and vegetarian, John Kellogg became superintendent in 1876 of the Seventh-Day Adventist Western Health Reform Institute, which then became the Battle Creek Sanitarium. William Kellogg developed numerous nut and vegetable products for his patients to eat, including cornflakes.

Cornflakes were not a new product, but they had never before been sold as a breakfast food. The Kellogg brothers began the Battle Creek Toasted Corn Flakes Company in 1906; it became known as the Kellogg Company.

HENRY FORD

ENGINEER AND ENTREPRENEUR

BORN: *July 30, 1863, Wayne County*
DIED: *April 7, 1947, Dearborn*

Born on a farm near Dearborn, Henry Ford worked as a machinist at the age of sixteen and later worked as an engineer. He became the leading manufacturer of American automobiles  in the early 1900s. He established the Ford Motor Company, which revolutionized the automobile industry with its assembly-line method of production. The savings from this technique helped Ford sell automobiles at a lower price than anyone had before. From 1908 to 1927 more than half the cars sold in the United States were Fords.

TY COBB
ATHLETE

BORN *December 18, 1886, Narrows, GA*
DIED *July 17, 1961, Atlanta, GA*

Although this baseball player was born in Georgia in 1886 and was nicknamed "The Georgia Peach," he was a Detroit Tiger outfielder for twenty-two seasons and then served as the team's manager for four years. He stole more bases and won more batting average titles than any other player of his era. Over the course of his twenty-four-season playing career in the American League, Cobb set records for runs scored and batting average. Cobb's mark of 892 stolen bases was beaten only in 1979, and his lifetime batting average of .366 was never equaled in the 1900s. Many people consider him the greatest offensive baseball player ever.

CHARLES AUGUSTUS LINDBERGH
AVIATOR

BORN *February 4, 1902, Detroit*
DIED *August 26, 1974, Maui, HI*

Lindbergh is best known for making the first nonstop solo flight across the Atlantic Ocean from New York to Paris, on May 20–21, 1927. In the monoplane *Spirit of St. Louis,* he made the flight in 33.5 hours.

Overnight, Lindbergh became a folk hero on both sides of the Atlantic and a well-known figure in most of the world. He died in 1974.

JOE LOUIS
ATHLETE

BORN *May 13, 1914, Lafayette, AL*
DIED *April 12, 1981, Las Vegas, NV*

Nicknamed "The Brown Bomber," Louis began his boxing career in Detroit at eighteen. He won his first professional fight in 1934. Both calm and quick, Louis won the heavyweight championship in 1937. After being defeated by Max Schmeling in 1936, Louis knocked the German boxer out in the first round of their 1938 rematch. In twelve years as heavyweight champ he scored twenty-one knockouts, defending his title twenty-five times. In his professional career he was defeated only three times in seventy-two fights.

THOMAS WELLER
PHYSICIAN

BORN *June 15, 1915, Ann Arbor*

Thomas Weller is a physician and virologist who was the corecipient (with John Enders and Frederick Robbins) of the Nobel Prize for physiology or medicine in 1954 for the successful cultivation of the poliomyelitis virus. This made it possible to study the virus "in the test tube" — a procedure that led to the development of a polio vaccine.

LEE IACOCCA
ENTREPRENEUR

BORN *October 15, 1924, Allentown, PA*

Lee Iacocca became famous when, as president and chairman of the board of the floundering Chrysler Corporation, he secured the largest amount of federal financial assistance ever given to a private corporation. He came to work for Chrysler in 1979 when the company had created a huge inventory of low-mileage cars at a time of rising fuel prices. The Chrysler Corporation then faced bankruptcy. Iacocca appealed to the federal government for aid, hoping that it would not allow Chrysler to fail when the national economy was already depressed. He was right. By 1981, after the government's help, Chrysler showed a small profit, and three years later it announced record profits of more than $2,400,000,000.

MALCOLM X
CIVIL RIGHTS ACTIVIST

BORN *May 19, 1925, Omaha, NE*
DIED *February 21, 1965, New York, NY*

Malcolm Little grew up in Lansing, Michigan, with a firsthand understanding of how difficult it was to be African American in the United States. His father was killed for urging blacks to end white mistreatment by returning to Africa.

　　While in jail for robbery, Malcolm discovered the Black Muslim religion. Once out of jail, he devoted himself to spreading The Nation of Islam. For a time he preached violence against whites and he changed his last name to "X," explaining that it reflected his lost African name. In 1964 he formed the Organization of Afro-American Unity, calling for blacks worldwide to join him in the fight against racism. In 1965 he was shot and killed at a rally in New York City.

ARETHA FRANKLIN
SINGER

BORN *March 25, 1942, Memphis, TN*

Born in Tennessee, Franklin moved to Detroit when she was six to live with her father, a minister. She began her singing career in gospel but at the age of eighteen switched to singing popular music with her father's permission. "I Never Loved a Man (the Way I Love You)" was her first song to sell a million copies. She mixed gospel with rhythm and blues and raised the style to new heights, eventually becoming known as the "Queen of Soul."

MADONNA
PERFORMER AND POP STAR

BORN *August 16, 1958, Bay City*

Born in 1958, Madonna Louise Ciccone became one of the twentieth century's greatest pop/rock stars. Her first hit, in 1983, was "Holiday." Over the next two decades, she explored a variety of musical genres and styles and is considered one of the first artists to take advantage of the music video. In the 1980s she also began an acting career. Her fame and power over her own career are matchless for a woman in the entertainment industry.

Michigan
History At-A-Glance

1673
Marquette and Jolliet begin their historic voyage from the shores of Lake Michigan.

1701
Detroit is founded by Antoine de la Mothe Cadillac.

1634
Jean Nicolet canoes through the Straits of Mackinac and along the Lake Michigan shore.

9000 B.C.
First Native Americans settle in Michigan.

1763
Treaty of Paris ending French and Indian War gives territory including what will become Michigan to Britain.

1783
The British cede the territory to the United States in the treaty ending the American Revolution.

1680s
The Iroquois and English enter the Straits of Mackinac; the French build forts there for the first time.

1805
Michigan Territory is created; Detroit made capital.

1614
The first Catholic missionaries settle in Michigan.

1671
The French lay formal claim to the lands of Michigan.

1600   **1700**   **1800**

1492
Christopher Columbus comes to New World.

1607
Capt. John Smith and three ships land on Virginia coast and start first English settlement in New World — Jamestown.

1754–63
French and Indian War.

1776
Declaration of Independence adopted July 4.

1787
U.S. Constitution written.

1773
Boston Tea Party.

1777
Articles of Confederation adopted by Continental Congress.

1812–14
War of 1812.

United States
History At-A-Glance

1825
New York's Erie Canal is completed, making it possible to transport goods by water from Detroit to New York City.

1837
Michigan becomes a state.

1847
Michigan's capital is moved to Lansing.

1894
Kellogg brothers make the first wheat flakes in Battle Creek, Michigan.

1896
Early experiments with "horseless carriages" in Michigan, leading to the rise of the automotive industry.

1910s
Ford's mass-production techniques revolutionize the automotive industry.

1930s
Labor unions of automotive workers become a powerful political force.

1936–37
United Auto Workers hold a sit-down strike in Flint.

1943
Race riot in Detroit.

1963
Michigan's constitution becomes the first to provide for a Department of Civil Rights.

1967
Race riot in Detroit.

1990s
Facing record losses, General Motors closes down several automotive plants in Michigan.

1800 — **1900** — **2000**

1848
Gold discovered in California draws 80,000 prospectors in the 1849 gold rush.

1861–65
Civil War.

1869
Transcontinental railroad completed.

1917–18
U.S. involvement in World War I.

1929
Stock market crash ushers in Great Depression.

1941–45
U.S. involvement in World War II.

1950–53
U.S. fights in the Korean War.

1964–73
U.S. involvement in Vietnam War.

2000
George W. Bush wins the closest presidential election in history.

2001
A terrorist attack in which four hijacked airliners crash into New York City's World Trade Center, the Pentagon, and farmland in western Pennsylvania leaves thousands dead or injured.

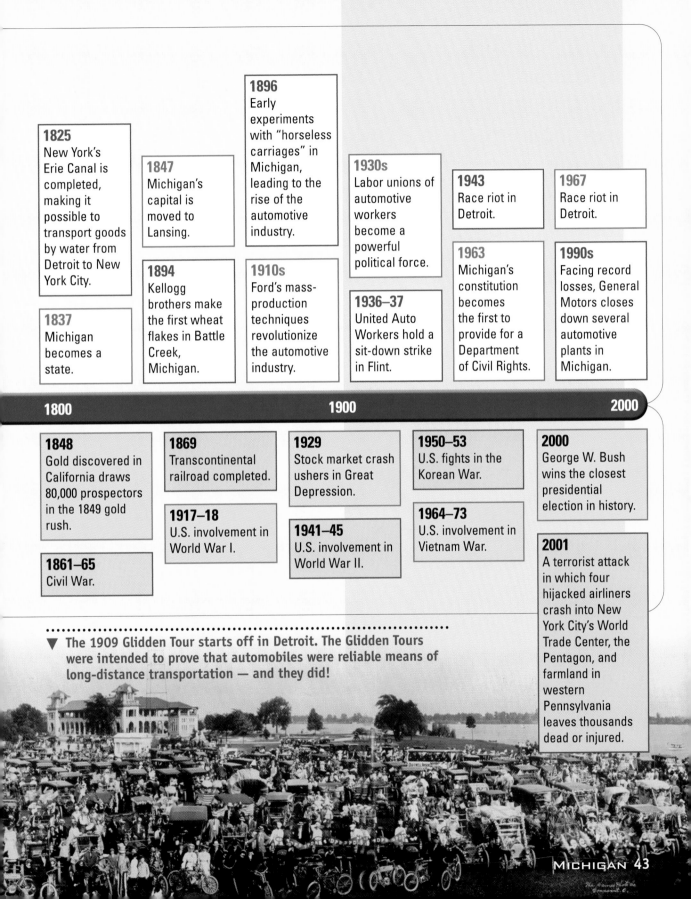

▼ The 1909 Glidden Tour starts off in Detroit. The Glidden Tours were intended to prove that automobiles were reliable means of long-distance transportation — and they did!

Festivals and Fun For All

Check web site for exact date and directions.

Ann Arbor Art Fair, Ann Arbor

Over one thousand artists make this fair the largest in the world. Juried artists, craftspeople, and musicians take over this college town for four days in the third week of July. Many locals plan vacations during this time to avoid crowds of over 500,000 art seekers and fairgoers.

www.artfair.org

Heritage Festival, Ypsilanti

A celebration of Michigan's heritage.
community.mlive.com/cc/heritagefestival

Womyn's Music Festival, Walhalla

One of the oldest women's music festivals in the U.S.

www.michfest.com/home.htm

National Cherry Festival, Traverse City

This seventy-year-old cherry festival is eight days long and attracts 500,000 people.
www.cherryfestival.org

Farmfest, Johannesburg

The best country, bluegrass, folk music, Irish music, blues, and reggae Northern Michigan has to offer.
www.farmhousemusic.org/farmfest

Coast Guard Festival, Grand Haven

A nationally recognized event sponsored by the United States Coast Guard.
www.ghcgfest.org

Tulip Time Festival, Holland

This ten-day festival draws well over one million visitors to the area each year.
www.tuliptime.org

Interlochen Arts Festival, Interlochen

Music, dance, and theater productions starring internationally renowned guest artists as well as talented Interlochen Arts Academy students and faculty.
www.interlochen.org

Henry Ford Museum & Greenfield Village, Dearborn

This outdoor village museum was a model for other such museums across the United States.
www.hfmgv.org/index2.html

Michigan State Fair, Detroit

Fun-filled fair events for everyone, every day!

www.mda.state.mi.us/statefair

Michigan Apple Festivals, various

Fall ushers in Michigan's annual festival season, in celebration of the state's most abundant fruit.

www.michiganapples.com/festivals2000.html

Common Ground Festival, Lansing

An annual celebration features an outstanding line-up of musical acts, focusing on top-level, national, contemporary music performers.

www.commongroundfest.com

East Lansing Film Festival, East Lansing

Watch independent and foreign features, documentaries, shorts, and student films from around the world.

www.elff.com

Detroit Jazz Festival, Detroit

The largest free jazz festival in North America!

www.detroitjazzfest.com

Festival, Grand Rapids

Six performance stages, singers, dancers, thespians, visual artists, and performers from all over western Michigan. It's the nation's largest all-volunteer arts event!

www.festival-gr.org

Morel Mushroom Festival, Boyne City

Celebrate the mushroom and participate in the mushroom-hunting championship.

www.morelfest.com

Michigan Brown Trout Festival, Alpena

A fishing competition and festival.

www.oweb.com/upnorth/btrout

The Sleeping Bear Dunegrass & Blues Festival, Empire

An outdoor musical feast of bluegrass, blues, and folk music held at the Sleeping Bear Dunes National Lakeshore.

www.leelanau.com/dunegrass

Books

Armbruster, Anne. *Lake Michigan: A True Book.* New York: Children's Press, 1997. The ecology and history of this Great Lake.

Fisher, Marcy Heller. *The Outdoor Museum: The Magic of Michigan's Marshall M. Fredericks.* Detroit: Wayne State University Press, 2001. Read about the art and life of world-famous sculptor and Michigander, the late Marshall M. Fredericks.

Gould, William. *Kellogg's.* New York: McGraw Hill, 1997. Find out how a nineteenth-century health fad led to the creation of a huge cereal company.

Kalbackacken, Joan. *Isle Royale National Park.* New York: Children's Press, 1997. Learn all about this 45-mile (72-km) archipelago with its submerged lands, shipwrecks, and abandoned copper mines.

Marsh, Carole. *Michigan Law for Kids: Don't Break It!* Peachtree City, GA: Gallopade Publishing Group, 1999. Discover the ins and outs of Michigan's legal system.

Stanley, Jerry. *Big Annie of Calumet: A True Story of the Industrial Revolution.* New York: Crown Publishers, 1999. Learn about one of the many battles over workers' rights that took place in the early twentieth century.

Wills, Charles A. *A Historical Album of Michigan.* Brookfield, CT: Millbrook Press, 1996. Learn more about Michigan's past, from the times before European settlement up to the present.

Web Sites

▶ Official Michigan State web site
www.michigan.gov

▶ Official Detroit web site
www.ci.detroit.mi.us

▶ The Library of Michigan
www.libofmich.lib.mi.us

▶ The Historical Society of Michigan
www.h-net.msu.edu/~hsm

▶ Michigan Parks and Recreation
www.ring.com/travel/parks.htm

Films

Glaser, Gary. *Gateway to Freedom: Detroit and the Underground Railway.* Troy, MI: Glaser Productions, Inc. 2000.